The Employee's Mentor

- Richard LaPalme -

According to the National Center for Education Statistics, each year in the United States approximately 1.2-million individuals receive 4-year degrees from colleges and universities. Another half-million receive masters, PhD's, and other various professional degrees. Most of these people will seek full-time employment with the goal of becoming career professionals. Until now, no one has written a book addressing their specific entry-level anxieties and needs. The Employee's Mentor is a concise practical guide to the first days, weeks, and months of professional employment.

Most newly minted graduates feel confident in the classroom, but have little idea what will be expected of them in the workplace. The Employee's Mentor explains the crucial differences between the academic and professional environments and the adjustments these differences require for success. The book also details how to communicate effectively in the workplace, as well as how to use each day to prepare for the reader's all-important initial performance evaluation. The Employee's Mentor demystifies the boss and clearly explains "how to manage your manager".

The Employee's Mentor

Richard LaPalme

To

John Tiffany

And

Robert Van Brocklyn

Contents

Introduction

Transitioning from school to your first career oriented job is one of America's great rites of passage in which we can each re-invent ourselves. Even if you were a less than diligent student, you need not despair regarding your chances for success in the workplace provided you become open to learning and adopt a serious work ethic. Be aware that workplace politics will always be a real and sometimes insurmountable phenomenon. However, there is still no place on earth where dedication, drive, and results pay off more than in the American workplace.

When I began my professional career, I naively expected that a senior executive would immediately take me under his or her wing and mentor me through the swift currents of my first years of employment. While no single individual filled this role at work, I was fortunate, back then, to play tennis regularly with a successful business executive who talked at length about the lessons he learned from his work world experiences. I also benefited, over the years, from wisdom imparted to me at work by various peers and managers, to whom I will remain ever grateful. However, I learned the most about succeeding at work by mentoring others. Early on, I designed and ran an entry-level training pool for the Information Systems division of Spalding Sporting Goods in Chicopee, Massachusetts. I found helping young people succeed at work as satisfying as coaching them to succeed on the tennis court. As my career progressed, I developed a reputation as an approachable individual, and consequently was able to advise many junior co-workers in their first years on the job.

Good mentors are hard to find, which is why I wrote this book to give the newly employed individual a practical concise reference for not just surviving, but thriving in today's highly competitive work world. Working hard in school is excellent preparation for success on the job;

however, it is not a guarantee by itself. A sound character and a hunger to learn are essential for success and are underlying themes throughout the following pages. When individuals who were successful students believe they can stop learning once they are hired, they quickly find themselves falling behind in their careers. Indeed, it's possible to encounter PhD's who lack awareness regarding what is going on in their organizations. Conversely, the work world contains many successful hard working people who did not graduate from college or tech school. Whatever their educational backgrounds, successful individuals usually share the attributes of honesty, energy, and a willingness to learn.

When the employer-employee relationship works, both parties benefit, wealth is created, and each side experiences a satisfaction that can truly be considered essential to the good life. My hope is that this book will enable you to make the most of the first year in your first full-time job, building a foundation for a successful career in your chosen field.

- Richard LaPalme

1

From Campus to Career

Knowing the crucial differences between life in school versus at the workplace will help you make needed adjustments to succeed on the job.

Whether you've just graduated from high school, community college, technical school, or a four-year university, there are important differences between the world you are leaving and the work world, or "real world", as it is sometimes called. Understanding these differences will help you transition into your first full-time job.

Most academic environments are homogeneous in terms of the people you encounter. While instructors may vary in age, most of your fellow / sister students were born within a few years of each other. Faculty and student body often share a similar world-view and set of personal goals. In most schools, the administration and teaching faculty, in exchange for some combination of tax dollars and tuition payments, are motivated to help you, the student, succeed. They design and promote an environment and tasks specifically for your development. Aside from an occasional study group, or as a welcome distraction from your studies, fellow / sister students usually have minimal impact on your day-to-day success. You are pretty much on your own. However, you are the principle product of the school, and its entire staff and facilities are designed to support your success.

In the work world, you usually encounter a heterogeneous population of individuals varying greatly in age, world-view, personal background, and goals. Managers and co-workers can have a huge impact on your success or failure. Tasks are real world in nature. With a few exceptions, when you report to work, employers usually do not have pre-analyzed approaches or solutions designed to help you develop your skills. Tasks are assigned simply because your organization needs to get them done to meet the organization's goals. *You are no longer the product that everything revolves around!*

Managers, co-workers, and you are now working towards real world goals – usually providing deliverables or services for profit or the public good. These goals are the products everyone and everything in the enterprise revolves around. In fact, employers will only pay you a salary if they believe that your efforts bring added value to the services or deliverables that you work on. If supporting your professional development by paying for your additional education and training promotes the organization's goals, great! Otherwise, the organization will have little incentive to invest in your professional growth. The linkage between the organization's goals and your professional growth may not always be apparent to your supervisors. You may sometimes have to sell the idea that your development in a particular area or skill will help promote the goals of the organization.

2
Have Yet to Land a Job?

What the author considers most important when applying for a professional position.

There are many good publications addressing this topic, and you may attend a school with a strong career development office that can prepare you for a successful job search. My goal, here, is not to be redundant, but to emphasize those few points that I've found particularly helpful, whether looking for work with a new employer, or posting for a new position within your existing place of employment.

First, you must determine the employer's job application process. Are you requested to apply in person? E-mail? Snail-mail? Some combination of the above? Do not fight the employer's process. Use any application forms or web sites provided. Be thoroughly honest and attach further documentation if a form doesn't provide you with the means to fully communicate your qualifications. Develop a concise cover letter, one page or less, tailored to each specific employer. Your letter must not look like a form letter.

Once you have submitted your application, contact the employer within a few days to confirm its receipt and to inquire regarding the next steps in the process. What is the time frame for filling the position? Can you call back in a week if you haven't heard anything? Will all applicants be notified whether or not they will be invited for an interview?

Be persistent. Call weekly, unless requested otherwise by the employer, to check on the status of your application. Some large employers throw away all outstanding applications on a monthly basis, especially for entry-level or trainee positions. This is done to help determine which applicants are still interested and which have found employment elsewhere. If you realize this to be the case, do not hesitate to reapply each month. It certainly won't be held against you.

When invited in for an interview, dress like the people who already work for the company or organization. If you are in any doubt that casual attire will be acceptable, dress up for the interview. For males, this means a dress shirt and necktie with either a suit or sport jacket. Females should likewise dress conservatively. Whether you dress casually or presidential, neatness in both clothes and grooming count.

Do some basic research on the organization prior to the interview. You can learn a lot from any web sites the employer sponsors. What is the basic mission of the employer? If the mission is not explicitly stated, make an intelligent guess. Be prepared to tell the employer how you would support this mission.

Be relaxed and friendly in the interview. The interviewer is a human being just like you. You probably won't know the details of the employer's operations, and most employers won't expect that you do. All employers, however, do look for honesty, ability to learn, and enthusiasm in potential employees. You should be prepared to talk about these three key areas in a personal way, citing examples from your life.

Develop a list of questions beforehand and bring it to the interview. Don't be afraid to ask questions such as, "Does senior management support this department's efforts?" Interviews should work both ways, allowing each side to learn what they need in order to make an informed decision. As soon as possible after the interview, send the people you met a thank-you note including any clarifications or additions to the interview that you would like to make.

Explore the use of employment agencies in your job search. Most agencies receive money from employers to recruit and screen potential employees before arranging interviews with the employer. Most will not take a fee from you, but will ask you to go to all the interviews that they arrange for you. This is good advice; however, do not hesitate to tell the agency when they are sending you to types of employers that don't interest you. Also, don't hesitate to sign up with more than one agency at a time, as long as you can make all the interviews multiple agencies arrange for you. If you feel an agency is wasting your time, consider ending your relationship with that agency. A good employment agency wants to match employees with employers in the most efficient manner possible.

Anecdote: Early in my data processing career, I accepted a job interview with a consulting firm in Farmington, Connecticut. This was an all day affair with several sessions, some involving multiple interviewers. By the end of the day, my head was spinning as I drove back to my home in Massachusetts. That evening, I had two very interesting phone calls. The first was from one of the consultants who interviewed me earlier that day. She told me that I didn't want to work for her firm. She said they brought in foreign workers on green cards and paid them substandard wages. She also said they often lied to clients regarding time frames and resources needed to complete assignments. A few minutes after we hung up, a second call came in. This time, it was a professional recruiter who worked for a local employment agency. He said that if I ever mentioned this phone call to anyone, he would deny that it took place. He then said that he heard about my interview earlier that day, and that, to protect my professional reputation, I should avoid future contact with that firm. By the time I went to bed, I had made up my mind to decline a second interview, should one be offered.

Anecdote: About the time of the above anecdote, I interviewed with a well known engineering firm. Again, I met several managers and staff during a day of two-way questions and answers. I couldn't say I was disappointed with anything anyone said, or that people weren't friendly enough for my liking, but I had a bad feeling about this place by the end of the day. I would sum it up by saying that everyone I spoke with exuded a grim determination regarding their work. I could tell that they were all under a great deal of pressure and, while I took my own work seriously, I doubted I could last long at this place without developing an ulcer.

Anecdote: Towards the end of a three-hour interview at a software development firm, I asked if upper management supported the efforts of the department that I would be working in. The two managers in the room confided that they were "working on that", but had a long way to go. They then asked if I was still interested in the job. When I said that I wasn't, I could feel their disappointment. I was about the tenth person they had interviewed for the position. While the two interviewers impressed me, I knew what it was like to work without support from senior management.

3
Day-to-Day Best Practices and Behaviors

Here are specific actions and behaviors to use for success each day on the job.

Truth or Consequences - The Indispensable Value of Honesty

All employers look for three core attributes in all employees:
- honesty / personal integrity
- aptitude or ability to learn
- energy and enthusiasm.

Honesty is by far the most important and most valued of the three. The other two attributes don't count for much if you are perceived as anything less than honest. In dealing with people, you must accept that perception is everything. You must deal with misunderstandings *as soon as you become aware of them*. It is not enough to tell yourself that you know the truth in a given situation and that's all that matters. If there is even a hint that someone you work with thinks you are less than honest, you must work to convince that person they are mistaken. Sometimes, this will mean a direct discussion of the matter in question. At other times, your reputation may only be restored by completing many successful transactions with a person over time. In either case, you have to guard your reputation as an honest person above all else! Trust is, after all, the foundation for all successful human relationships.

Winning Friends and Influencing People - Emotional Bank Accounts

Even if you are honest, competent, and enthusiastic, unless people enjoy your company (i.e. "like" you), your chances for success are greatly diminished in most organizations. If you feel "likeability challenged", the following discussion should help you gain confidence in this key area of human relations.

Steven Covey, the author of "The Seven Habits of Highly Successful People", talks about the concept of an emotional bank account. Simply put, when you meet someone for the first time, each party's emotional bank account regarding the other is set at zero. As time progresses, you each make deposits and withdrawals in each other's emotional bank accounts based on the way you treat each other. For example, providing useful information or paying a compliment counts as a deposit. False information or rudeness translates into a withdrawal. At work, you can rarely afford to have anyone's emotional bank account regarding you become overdrawn. Relationships can survive the occasional bad day provided there is a wealth of deposits in each party's emotional bank account regarding the other. Those deposits having been accrued over prior days, weeks, and months. From day one on your first job, be aware of how you treat everyone you encounter. Start making positive contributions in everyone's emotional bank accounts. There will be days when, out of either carelessness or necessity, you will make withdrawals from co-workers' emotional bank accounts. You want to make sure that your relationships can survive those withdrawals.

Telling it Like it is - Assertive Communication and Behaviors

One of the most valuable concepts I learned in graduate school involved the true meaning of assertiveness. If you can attend a class or seminar on assertiveness training involving in-class practice through role playing, do so. The effort will pay off many times over when you begin your career, and throughout your life, both in and out of the work world. I will attempt below to explain this valuable concept.

In explaining assertive behavior, it helps to spend some time describing common behaviors that are *not* assertive. Assertiveness is not, in any way, aggressive behavior. Sarcasm, yelling, threatening words, or body language are all forms of aggressive behavior and are all aimed at bullying a person. Aggressive behavior always results in large withdrawals from a person's emotional bank account regarding the aggressor. Likewise, assertiveness is not in any way passive or meek behavior. Speaking in a small hard-to-hear voice, acting scared or inferior, or framing everything in terms designed to make the other person feel sorry for you are all forms of passive behavior. Passive behavior often leads people to lose respect, a type of emotional bank account withdrawal, for the person acting passively. People often unconsciously become passive when they are genuinely scared or lack confidence.

Both aggressive and passive behaviors are intended to manipulate people. They can sometimes get desired results at the high cost of depleting emotional bank accounts that you have with other individuals.

How do you communicate problematic information to peers and bosses in a way that is positive to your relationships? The answer is the direct honest style of communication known as assertiveness. Looking people in the eye, firm handshakes, controlled yet expressive tone of voice, and confident non-accusatory speech are all hallmarks of assertive behavior. Assertive communication avoids undertones of either bullying or "sucking up". In an assertive conversation, neither party cuts off the other's sentences, nor tries to dominate. When both parties are assertive, a high level of communication, respect, and understanding are usually the result. The challenge is to remain assertive even when the other person resorts to passive and / or aggressive behaviors. There are times when the other person will attempt to lure you out of the assertive world of logic and mutual respect and into the emotionally charged world of accusation and impulsive argument. In such situations, you will need to do your best to remain calm while deciding whether it is worth continuing the conversation, or whether it is best to close it off for at least the time being.

It is important to understand that assertive speech, while controlled, does not mean emotionless or monotone speech. In an assertive manner, you can tell someone that you have a problem with them, or that some recent event is causing you concern or even anger. In so doing, there is nothing wrong with the other person seeing that you are either upset or deeply concerned about something. The key is conveying your concern without either trying to bully or curry favor with the other person. Again, it helps to read about this valuable concept, but it is best acquired through seeing it in action in a classroom setting, if possible.

Anecdote: My company initiated a suggestion program in which each departmental vice president was obligated to discuss suggested procedural changes with the submitting team. My team suggested that when an analyst developed a recommendation, the analyst must be advised regarding the ultimate disposition of the recommendation. It was our experience that after putting in long hours developing an idea, we were rarely told what the reactions were as our document went up the management chain. This made it difficult, if not impossible, for us to gain insight into management's point of view and make relevant adjustments to future recommendations.

As required, we were invited to attend a meeting on this idea in a nearby conference room. We assembled at the appointed time and waited for our VP to arrive. Twenty minutes later, just as we were all about to leave, he did so with a flourish. Striding to an empty chair, he pulled it back from the table and proceeded to sit on the top of the seatback, placing his feet on the chair's seat! (Don't try this at home – I was amazed that he didn't lose his balance!) Duly ensconced, and looking down upon the rest of us, he barked, "So what's the big problem anyway?" The session went straight downhill from there. In those first few seconds, he made it clear to all in the room that he was the boss, and that the idea on the table was dead on arrival. By his aggressive behavior, the VP made a huge withdrawal from everyone's emotional bank account regarding him. While it was clear this didn't bother him in the least, his ability to get productive ideas from his staff was in steep decline. Instead of engaging in a good-faith assertive discussion of the idea, he seemed determined to shut down communication. As you can imagine, no more ideas were suggested by my team during the rest of the suggestion program, or thereafter.

Anecdote: I once worked for a manager who used physical contact to establish dominance over his workers. He would often grab your arm while asking you for an ad-hoc status report. Once, he even pulled on my necktie, in passing, while I was talking to a co-worker who rolled her eyes in disgust. After my first week of experiencing this tactic, I decided that I would have to do something about it before I reflexively "touched" him back in a most non-assertive manner! I didn't want to embarrass him in front of other people. Well, actually, I would have loved to, but knew it would be a self-defeating way of dealing with the problem. Instead, I waited until we were alone and asked him if he remembered a few instances of his grabbing my arm. When he acknowledged what I was referring to, I assertively told him that I really didn't appreciate being touched that way, and that I was asking him not to do so in the future. His jaw dropped a little. He said that he understood, and that he wouldn't grab my arm going forward. While he definitely seemed surprised, he also seemed to appreciate my speaking to him about this in private. Still, I had an up and down relationship with him, as did just about everyone else I knew, during the remaining time that I worked for him. But at least the arm grabbing stopped, and my blood pressure lowered.

As illustrated in the above anecdote, no one is clairvoyant – don't assume people can read your mind when you are anxious or even angry about something. If you feel your manager needs to know about the problems you are having with a sick child, or the person who sits next to you, you need to meet with the manager and have a clear and frank discussion. If your manager has to cut the meeting short for any reason, reschedule to make sure your message is fully received. Sometimes, putting things in writing is necessary if the manager is not a good listener. However, always be very careful when putting issues in writing, as you can never effectively take a written statement back! Read your message over several times. Place yourself in your manager's shoes, making sure your text has neither a passive nor aggressive tone. The written word has neither facial expression nor tone of voice, and therefore can be easily misinterpreted, if not totally misunderstood. If the message is at all sensitive, it is best to arrange a face-to-face verbal discussion, if possible.

Speak to Actions, Not Motives

When you speak or write about difficult issues involving peers or managers, only speak to behaviors – do not address motives. Unless a person explicitly states his or her motives, it can make you look highly presumptuous to state what you think they are. Also, you can easily be off base, which can make you look petty and immature. You may think Fred is out to get you, when actually his close friend just died and he's having a really bad time dealing with it. This doesn't make Fred's behavior excusable. However, it may be more understandable than you might portray by declaring motivations that only hurt relationships all around. If you stick to discussing behaviors, you're likely to retain everyone's respect, and avoid emotionally charged misunderstandings. If your manager asks why you think Fred is behaving in a certain way, simply say that you can't guess what motivates Fred, you can only talk to what Fred is doing and how it effects you.

There are times when your perceptions regarding motivations are welcome by your peers and managers, and that is when analyzing clients or competitors. Indeed, this type of "psyching out" may become an important part of your job! However, as stated previously, when speaking about your peers or managers, be careful not to state what you think is going on inside their heads!

Beware the Heat of the Moment

Avoid acting or speaking when you become seriously angry. Give yourself a chance to cool off, even if it means taking a walk or waiting until the next day so you can really think things through.

Anecdote: I once worked for a manager who took everything very seriously, which could make him upset about something on a frequent basis. He was often seen walking in the parking lot during work hours. In talking to him about this, he told me that he had learned the hard way to take a walk and cool down to avoid popping off inappropriately to a co-worker or superior. While his frequency of employing this tactic seemed excessive, the basic idea is a good one.

Get to the Point!

In both written and verbal communication, always give the punch line first and then proceed to supporting details if, and only if, you feel they help the listener understand what he or she needs to know. To reverse the order, saving the point to last, usually annoys your listener and risks losing his or her attention. If supporting details illustrate how well you coped with a difficult situation, consider saving them for your weekly written status or annual Performance Evaluation.

Do Not Inherit Another Employee's Baggage

Sometimes, a prior employee did something on a regular basis that bothered your manager so much, you may find him or her repeatedly telling you not to do a certain action, that "Fred used to do that all the time and it drove me crazy". This can happen whether or not you've actually mimicked Fred's behavior. You need to remind your manager, in a good natured assertive way, that you are not Fred, and to please not let Fred's annoying past cloud your manager's judgment of your performance.

Take Ownership of Problems and Requests

This book contains much detail regarding how to handle manager assigned tasks (see Chapter 6). However, it's not unusual to receive many requests, large and small, for your time and effort from clients, co-workers, and other managers within your organization. Unless your manager tells you to handle such requests in another manner, you should always get back to the requestor as soon as possible, telling him or her what your course of action will be. This should include giving an estimate of how long it will take to fulfill their request. Or, if someone else is more appropriate to do the work being requested, bring that person together with the requestor, making sure they both agree to continue on the task without your involvement. If you are the right person, but are up to your ears in work, tell the requestor that, because of your current workload, you cannot, at this time, estimate a time frame for task resolution. The bottom line is to make sure the requestor is quickly informed of your intentions and that he or she, as well as your manager, receive weekly updates on your progress. Requestors would rather quickly hear that you are too busy to immediately help them than to be wondering whether you've received their request. Whatever your course of action, make sure to communicate with all concerned parties early and often. You want to be known as a person who quickly responds to being contacted; whether or not you have an immediate answer, or can spend time on the issue you've been sent.

Anecdote: Working in a computer application development / support role at a large company usually limited me to dealing with clients within the organization. However, one day when my phone rang, I was surprised to find myself speaking with a parish priest in another state who was trying to make sure that an insurance premium had made it to the home office on time to maintain coverage. How he got connected to me was a mystery. I could have easily said "not my job" and transferred his call back to the main switchboard. However, I knew that this would not help him. So I took his name and telephone number and told him that either I, or someone from my company, would get back to him soon, hopefully by day's end. I next contacted the customer support call centers within the company to determine which one could provide the priest with the status of his premium payment. Once I found the appropriate call center, I obtained assurance that they would immediately contact the priest. I then called the priest back and encouraged him to call the call center number if he wasn't contacted soon. This was as far as I went. I could also have called the priest within a few days to make sure he had obtained the desired information. Why go through all of this when the customer was connected to me by mistake in the first place? I believed it was always in my interests to have my company's customers get issues resolved with the least amount of hassle.

Multitasking and Time Management

Even new employees are often required to tackle several tasks at once. Multitasking is a real challenge and requires strong organizational skills to avoid simply spinning your wheels with little or no results. Learn any time management software provided by your employer and take full advantage of it. If no software is provided, or, as a supplement, purchase a hard copy day planner at a business supply store and use its features. Regularly prioritize your assignments and plan your time accordingly. Document priorities in your written statuses. Review priorities with your manager at one-on-one status meetings. Regularly check on low priority requests to see if they are still needed.

Multitasking means you often have to stop work on a specific assignment to attend to other tasks / emergencies. When this happens, and it often will, do not rely on your memory. Document what you've accomplished whenever you have to stop working on a given task. This will save valuable time, not to mention your mental health, when you are able to return to it.

4
Managing Your Manager

This chapter includes detailed information on the Performance Evaluation Process including specific employee actions to optimize your PE rating.

What do I mean by the term "managing your manager?" In simple terms, it means getting him or her to clearly communicate requirements for your short-term assignments and long-term career advancement, and to reward you appropriately when you meet those requirements. It also entails making sure your manager allocates adequate time and resources to enable you to accomplish your assignments.

Managing your manager involves constant communication. This is often easier said than done. However, it is crucial for your success on the job, and something you will find yourself devoting considerable time and energy doing. The annual PE, or Performance Evaluation Process, is an invaluable tool for you to accomplish this goal.

There is nothing more frustrating than finding yourself in the middle of your annual performance evaluation without being prepared. To your horror, you discover that your manager and you are not on the same wavelength regarding your value to the organization. He or she seems oblivious to what you have accomplished during the prior year. Or, just as bad, you find yourself being evaluated by someone who just replaced your first manager who left the company four weeks ago, and neither of you have documentation for the prior forty-eight weeks! A lackluster performance review usually results, accompanied by a modest raise in pay, if any. *Do not let this happen to you. If you read nothing else in this book, study the following information on the Performance Evaluation Process and put it into practice beginning day one on your new job.*

While some employers lack a formal way to evaluate employee performance, most employ a Performance Evaluation Process composed of several distinct phases covering a twelve-month period. Most such processes are intended to support a "no surprises" environment regarding career advancement and are structured more or less as follows.

Performance Evaluation (PE) Process *Overview*

Part I – Written agreement regarding goals / expectations followed by weekly / bi-weekly written statuses and one-on-one meetings to discuss progress.

Part II – 6 month or mid-term check-up followed by weekly / bi-weekly written statuses and one-on-one meetings to discuss progress.

Part III – 12 month final performance evaluation including discussion of possible merit salary increase and /or bonus.

If a formal PE process exists on paper, you should make sure, as much as possible, that it actually happens. Some managers are diligent about scheduling and completing PE components during the year, either because they believe in its benefits, or because their boss does. However, you'll be surprised how many managers take this essential process lightly.

Performance Evaluation (PE) Process *Detail*

Part I – Written agreement regarding goals / expectations: The PE Process should begin very soon (within a week) after you are hired. If your manager is dragging his or her feet in setting up a meeting to discuss your goals and objectives for the upcoming year, you should ask him or her if you can schedule the meeting. If resistance is still encountered, *or if no formal PE process exists,* you should do your best to document your understanding of your goals and objectives, and submit a written document to your manager for approval, or at least comment. To be effective, a PE Part I should document at least the following six major topics and subtopics:

1. The coming year's goals for the

- organization / company
- division / department
- team
- employee / you (usually 4 or 5 specific goals or major tasks with time frames for completion – clearly written so that it will be easy to determine whether you have accomplished them).

2. Your manager's current requirements for acceptable performance in your job at your current job grade.

3. Your manager's current requirements for promotion to the next job grade.

4. Agreement that you will submit either weekly or bi-weekly written statuses that will at least cover

- accomplishments for the period covered
- any tasks that are behind schedule
- issues that need manager's input / action
- planned vacation days in foreseeable future (usually for the next month).

5. Training

- your specific training needs
- training resources available to you, both in-house and third-party
- how will training be arranged, and by whom?

6. Agreement between you and your manager to communicate *as soon as possible* when a problem becomes apparent to either party. You can only make adjustments regarding issues or problems that you are informed about.

A special word regarding training: No matter what technical training your job may require, in today's work world, just about everyone can benefit from training in 1) Presentation Skills, 2) Business Writing, 3) Time Management, and 4) Negotiation Skills. I would also recommend training in Assertive Communication and Steven Covey's Seven Habits of Highly Successful People, if possible.

Once the PE Part I issues and goals have been documented and signed by both employee and employer, regular meetings are scheduled and held to discuss progress towards, and any needed changes in them. These weekly or bi-weekly meetings are crucial. Don't let them be rescheduled out of existence, or you will begin to lose assurance that you and your manager are on the same page – a sure road to unpleasant surprises including career derailment! At these regular meetings, you should be discussing any issues raised by your written statuses, as well as whether you and your manager have any issues relative to anything documented in your PE Part I. Have any goals changed? Are you on track regarding your personal goals? If not, what can you and / or your manager do to put things back on track? If you and your manager approach these meetings in good faith, there should be no surprises when it comes time to discuss salary and bonuses at the end of the PE cycle.

IMPORTANT: On a daily basis, keep an ongoing file of accomplishments, issues, relevant e-mails, status reports, etc. to help document what might otherwise slip through the cracks as time goes on. It's easy to forget things when writing your status report late on a Friday. Likewise, your manager may sometimes need added documentation to educate him or her regarding events that he or she did not witness.

Part II – The mid-term check-up: Roughly six months after completing the PE Part I, you and your manager should meet to conduct and document a mid-term check-up. This is a formal way to insure that the parties are still in agreement regarding all the issues discussed in the PE Part I, including any changes that were agreed to since the PE Part I. Hence, the agenda for the PE Part II is the Part I document plus any intervening changes. *In the PE Part II, the manager should put in writing his or her brief assessment of how well the employee is doing towards achieving the personal goals established at the beginning of the PE cycle.*

Once the above PE Part II has been documented and signed by both parties, regular meetings are scheduled and held to discuss weekly written statuses, as well as progress towards the employee's goals, training issues, and the possible need for any changes in course. Again, these weekly / bi-weekly meetings are crucial. Without them, it is easy for your relationship with your boss to break down, especially in large organizations. You should continue to keep an ongoing file of accomplishments and relevant documentation, just as you've been doing all year.

Part III – The year's final evaluation: Six months after the Part II, and one year after the Part I, the PE Part III is held in which manager and employee formally document how the prior twelve months went in terms of goals and training achieved. The final "grade" or rating should be no surprise if the PE process was performed as described above, in good faith, by both parties throughout the year's PE cycle. In many organizations, the employee is required to "go first" by putting his or her evaluation of how he / she achieved Part I goals in writing, and submitting his / her conclusions to the manager. Within a short time (no more than a week), the manager submits a written response to the employee, addressing each of the employee's goals and major assignments, along with an overall rating for the year's work, such as "Met all requirements" or "Met some but not all requirements", etc. Then a formal meeting is held for the parties to discuss their respective points of view and the reasons why they hold them. It sometimes happens that a manager may modify his or her written evaluation based on issues raised by the employee at this meeting. However, in most instances, the Part III Final Report stands with few or no changes and is the basis for deciding any raises (a.k.a. "performance increases") and / or bonuses.

When writing your year-end self-evaluation, keep in mind that this is no time for modesty or understatement. You have to fully explain and sell your accomplishments, using any and all documentation which you've accumulated during the year. Some managers keep detailed folders on each employee as the year progresses and some, believe it or not, don't. In many instances, the only way your manager will remember or become aware of what you have done eight months ago is through reading about it in your self-evaluation. A common mistake made by new employees is to understate their accomplishments in written self-evaluations assuming their manager will make up the difference in his or her written evaluation of the employee. They rarely do. It is better to risk overstating what you have done then to understate. If your manager feels you have overdone things in your self-evaluation, a useful discussion will often ensue which will help both sides gain insight into the other's point of view.

At the conclusion of Part III, a manager may be able to tell you whether you will be receiving a salary increase or bonus. Often, more time is needed to determine salary and bonus decisions. Whether or not you receive a raise is not just a function of your final PE rating. It also depends upon whether your organization made money or accomplished other goals during the year, and just how many dollars have been, or will be, allocated to your department and team. Likewise, an outstanding PE does not automatically result in promotion to the next job grade level. A lot depends on whether there are openings above you to fill. Do not be afraid to ask detailed questions of your manager, or manager's higher up the chain, regarding criteria for raises and promotions. You cannot afford to remain ignorant about these key issues. What you are told, as well as not told, will speak volumes regarding how your organization handles career advancement within its ranks.

When reading your manager's evaluation of you, or engaging in related discussions with your manager, it's not unusual for other employee's names to come up as a matter of documentation if they were key players in tasks or goals involving you. However, in no circumstance should your manager directly compare your performance to that of another employee's. Doing so is unprofessional. It's unfair to you and violates the confidentiality of the person you are being compared to. If this happens, try and get the manager to focus on your performance as compared to established standards and requirements for the job, not as compared to other specific individuals. After all, what other employees do, and how they do it, are often not visible to you, and can frequently change. You deserve to be judged against written requirements that have been pre-agreed to by you and your manager.

Whatever you receive for your final Performance Evaluation rating, you must reconcile with it as you and your manager begin the entire Performance Evaluation Process again for the upcoming year.

5
Who is the Manager?

Next to your own effort and judgment, your manager will be the most important factor in your day-to-day happiness and professional success or failure.

Before I began my professional career, my image of the boss / manager / supervisor was shaped largely by what I had experienced in movies and literature. In my mind, the boss was someone who had worked his or her way up from the ground floor of the organization, and therefore knew in detail each aspect of the job his or her people did. He or she valued each employee and wanted to develop people to their greatest potentials. Amazingly, I have actually encountered a few bosses like this in my career – one of them is named in this book's dedication. However, reality regarding managers must take into account that many organizations believe you don't have to have experience doing a job in order to effectively manage people in that job. My experience reporting directly to over thirty different managers in my career indicates otherwise. The best managers effectively talk the talk because they once walked the walk. You may envision the boss as someone who was chosen from many qualified candidates, likes people, and has studied the science of managing both projects and employees. In reality, he or she may be in the boss's chair simply because no one else raised their hands when senior management asked who would like to try a management position! This person may have received little or no training or support as a manager, may not particularly like people, but simply desires the extra pay received for managing. Indeed, managers throughout the public and private sectors vary greatly in their abilities and competence.

In summary, your manager is a person who *may, or may not...*
- have experience doing the job you do.
- know the company well.
- be interested in your professional development.
- have experience or training as a manager.
- receive support and encouragement from his or her manager.

- be in the position as the result of a pains-taking evaluation and selection process.
- be in the position simply because he or she raised his/her hand when it was asked who would like to try management!

Your manager may be good at most parts of his / her job, but may be a poor staff developer. In many organizations, managers are *not* specifically rewarded for how well they develop the people under them.

All managers have their good and bad days. They are not machines. Managers have lives and pressures outside of work that can leak into their dealings with you. Of course, all the above also holds true for you and your co-workers! Try not to carry each day's baggage / pettiness forward if at all possible. As trite as it may sound, try to make each day a fresh start on the job.

Anecdote: The respected CEO of a large successful company used to address all employees as "associates" and began each in-house presentation with recognition of how important the employees were to the company's success. For the most part, the company's work environment reflected the CEO's attitude toward employees. Managers were expected to lay out specific unambiguous requirements for job success, and to recognize when those requirements were met or exceeded. Poor performance was dealt with on an individual basis via the annual Performance Evaluation Process. For the most part, associates felt valued and respected. Consequently, even if salaries were sometimes greater elsewhere, most people felt a high degree of loyalty to the company. If the company did well in a given year, bonus dollars were distributed to *all* employees in direct proportion to their salaries except for those on probation for performance issues. The assumption being that an individual's salary was the cumulative result of his or her annual performance evaluations and therefore accurately reflected that person's relative worth to the organization.

This all changed when a successor CEO took over. The new leader believed that, aside from himself and a few of his direct reports, everyone else in the company was expendable and could be replaced, at will, without the company being harmed. Hence, staff turnover was to be strongly encouraged in order to lower overall salary and benefit costs. The "associate" label was deliberately dropped. Managers throughout the company were told that the CEO assumed there was "dead wood" in each department and team. At a company-wide management meeting, the CEO wondered aloud what good managers were to him if they couldn't identify, and eliminate, the bottom five-percent of their respective organizations each year. Subsequently, an annual culling of five-percent of each team's staff became a management expectation regardless of how effective team members actually were.

The effects on the company's practices and culture were immediate and profound. Managers within a department were directed to meet annually to rank all departmental employees across teams according to perceived effectiveness. An employee's ranking depended on his or her manager's ability to defend the employee's work to other managers whom often didn't understand the goals and obstacles specific to the employee being ranked. Annual bonus dollars were awarded entirely to the top five-percent of ranked employees, making the rankings worth many thousands of dollars to a select few individuals. This was called the "Star System". The rest of the staff, regardless of the value they added to the company during the year, received nothing from the bonus pool. The practice of managers spontaneously calling each other to give input (i.e. complain) about staff members was encouraged and, in many cases, employed as a means to develop ammunition for the annual employee rankings. It quickly became obvious that if your advancement as a manager was tied to the perceived effectiveness of your people, one way to raise your team's image (and your own chances for promotion) was to regularly criticize rival manager's and their employees. Also, as managers perceived they had to find one or more team members each year to fire, they backed away from their staff, and increasingly became vague in their requirements for success, both in regards to specific tasks / projects and career advancement. Everyone was simply told that they needed to forever "raise the bar" in order to survive. This made it possible to tell somebody that they just didn't measure up, no matter what deliverables they produced. Morale dropped severely and resignations increased as people could no longer see how to succeed within the organization other than to curry favor with perceived power brokers.

On one hand, cronyism flourished as who you were "in" with began to heavily outweigh how effective you were at your job. On the other hand, managers evaded accountability by embracing vague work requirements, and by ceasing to collaborate with their workers as well as with each other. Finger pointing regarding most day-to-day tasks became the norm. Trust went out the door along with mutual respect and loyalty. Employees saw themselves in no-win situations as the mandatory winnowing of staff began via layoffs and firings. New people were hired weekly to fill resulting voids. Soon, over two-thirds of the employees had less than two years experience with the organization. The ability to support daily operations was coming into question! From the time of his arrival until about six years into his reign, when the board of directors fired the CEO for purportedly unrelated abuse of power issues, salary alone became the only factor that kept most people working at the company.

The current CEO is trying to return the company to a more worker friendly environment in order to keep the remaining experienced staff from leaving in disgust. He specifically mentions the need to return to a meritocracy, a place where results matter more than personal connections.

There is no way to accurately measure how badly the company was hurt by its recent encounter with the "employees as commodity" high turnover strategy, but its current CEO seems to realize that the price was high indeed.

This story illustrates a wide range of manager appreciation of employees, from highly appreciative, to not at all. The best managers treat people as individuals, seeing over time which ones are dedicated and which ones need external motivation. There are managers, however, that assume all employees will shortchange the company whenever possible, and constantly need to be pressured in order to perform. The problem with this approach is that most (but not all) employees take pride in their work and put a certain amount of pressure on themselves to perform. The cynical manager doesn't recognize this and, as a matter of course, piles more pressure on all of his or her employees. Such pressure is additive: the five pounds of pressure you put on yourself, combined with the four pounds added by the boss, add up to nine pounds of pressure, only four of which are visible to your manager. This results in a highly stressful situation which can lead to physical illness and impaired job performance. Sometimes, you can educate the manager regarding your level of dedication and the negative effects of his or her added pressure. Unfortunately, managers who operate in this fashion often are not the most insightful or caring individuals. Even people who otherwise are excellent bosses must adhere to the corporate culture being promoted by senior management. When the new CEO in the above anecdote required the elimination of five-percent of each team annually, many good people in middle and frontline management positions had to decide whether to support the process or leave the company. Some did leave. Others had to deal with the realities of supporting their families in a tight job market, and therefore carried out the CEO's directives as best they could.

Anecdote: One of the best bosses I ever experienced happened to be the first person I reported to on my first career oriented job. I was working in a production support environment which, from time-to-time, could rapidly turn upside-down. When it did, this manager would gather the team and say, "Everyone, try to remain calm. Keep in mind that one-hundred years from now, no one will remember anything about what we are doing here today. Now, let's roll up our sleeves, put our thinking caps on, and see how we can turn this situation around!" The message was simple, but powerful. We all felt that this man was behind us, and was trying to optimize our chances to succeed by not over pressuring us into making mistakes. He fully realized that whatever mess we were in was more than enough motivation to inspire total effort. Everyone on the team really loved this guy and would do whatever we could to make him look good.

The bottom line is that managers, like all people, are highly complex and varied individuals. The more you can learn about your manager's background, abilities, and beliefs, the better you will be able to effectively support him or her as well as sell him or her on your value to the organization.

6

Manager Assigned Tasks

What follows are several specific behaviors that will help you shorten your learning curve whenever you take on an assignment.

Micromanagers and How to Work For Them

Some managers will give you a list of highly specific things to do without giving you any overall goal or context. Beware - you have entered the realm of the micromanager! Occasionally, a better manager may resort to this tactic in an emergency, when time does not allow him or her to give you the background and overall goal related to the assigned tasks. Unless time is of the essence, you need to ask the micromanager what the ultimate goal is, so that you can intelligently react to obstacles. If you simply start performing a laundry list of tasks without knowing why you are doing them, adding value or reacting intelligently will be next to impossible when something or someone blocks your way. You'll always have to go back to the manager to have him or her suggest alternate approaches, thus making yourself appear less competent. Don't let this happen to you. Always ask what the ultimate goal is, or what end-result is desired, upon receiving an assignment.

The Need to Often Ask Questions

Hopefully, most of the time, you will be given the ultimate goal or desired deliverable and be expected to use your own judgment on how to achieve it. This is when most jobs become fulfilling, as you are able to use your back-ground and judgment to engage in independent action. When receiving such an initial assignment, don't hesitate to ask questions. Real world tasks aren't figured out in advance like school assignments unless, in some rare instances, when they are doubling as a training exercise. If you were a high achiever in school, you may sometimes find it difficult to ask questions of your manager. High achieving students often hesitate to ask for more information because they learned early in their education that their teacher had usually provided all necessary information in the introduction to their assignments. Asking for more information only resulted in being told that they already had all the information needed, and to simply "get to it!"

The work world is very different. Your manager usually has not figured out in advance how to do the task he or she has assigned you, and won't be surprised if you ask a few clarifying questions before you begin. Be specific with your questions. You need to feel as though you understand the manager's requirements thoroughly before you begin the task. Are there documented company standards regulating how deliverables must be produced, or what qualities / attributes the assigned deliverable needs to conform to? If you are asked to develop a complex deliverable, is there a documented Product Development Life Cycle required for use in its development? Such life cycles can include several phases: Planning, Analysis, Design, Construction, Testing, Implementation, Production and Ongoing Maintenance, and Sun Setting or Decommissioning. If you are newly hired, who can you use as a mentor and information source if you have technical questions?

Anecdote: One of the most challenging and interesting positions I ever held was as the Standards Coordinator for the Information Systems division of a large insurance company. As a non-manager, I had the responsibility, often with understated management support, to assemble and coordinate a regularly meeting standards committee composed of middle to senior managers from the division's various IS support and application departments. Our goal was to determine which hardware, software, application development, and application support best practices needed to be documented and published for the various computing platforms within the company. Once published, we were to maintain these best practices as management endorsed standards and procedures, including procedures for their enforcement throughout the Information Systems Division.

The premise of this massive effort was that it is a fundamental responsibility of management to be stewards of company resources, such as the information computing infrastructure, by using them in optimally productive and cost effective ways. Towards that end, it was imperative that management clearly communicate to all employees when certain infrastructure components, either hardware or software, must be used in certain ways, or when certain steps must be used to ensure the quality of IS deliverables.

Most managers liked the *idea* of publishing standards and procedures. It jumpstarted the training of new employees and provided a way to leverage lessons learned in one area out to the entire organization. It greatly simplified support and maintenance of automated systems once they were in production (in non-standardized shops each system is often a unique world unto itself). The problems arose when dealing with issues of enforcement. Traditional quality control requires managers to document rationale and literally sign their names when exceptions to published standards and procedures are taken in order to satisfy a client's unique business need. The benefits are threefold: 1) the standards committee can see how the standards work in the real world and modify them when necessary, 2) people coming on to the project midstream can see what compliance exceptions were taken, and why, going back to the project's beginning, and 3) accountability for compliance decisions is identified with a specific manager who can then be judged on the appropriateness of his or her decisions come evaluation time.

The one word managers like to use the most about themselves is "accountable", yet many managers balked at the idea of having to sign their names when exceptions to standards were being made. Mind you, it wasn't as if we were telling them that they couldn't make such decisions. They were being empowered to do just that. However, we were telling them that they couldn't keep their compliance decisions a secret from the rest of the company! The better managers recognized this and backed the quality control effort. Sadly, some managers resisted, labeling it as "overkill" or "bureaucracy". They really wanted to be able to point fingers elsewhere if their poorly made compliance decisions resulted in production problems or deliverables that needed reworking.

Active Listening

Whether your manager employs micro or macro management, you need to continually develop your listening skills. Active listening means occasionally nodding and offering a comment, now and then, to indicate that you understand what is being conveyed. If the speaker allows, interject when you need something repeated or further explained. You will get clearer information, and the speaker will gain confidence that you understand him or her, while learning over time how to better explain things to you. If you sit there like a stone, the speaker can walk away wondering if you got anything that was said. Or, worse, assume that you understood everything clearly, when you actually missed several key points but were afraid to ask questions.

Taking Notes is a Good Thing

Don't be afraid to take written notes in meetings with managers or co-workers. In fact, whenever you are called into your boss's office, or anyone else's office, you should bring along paper and pen for note taking. Some people are machinegun like when dispensing information, even after being asked to slow down. Write down as much as you can while they are talking, unless explicitly asked not to. Then, do a brain-dump on paper immediately after such an information filled meeting. Don't be afraid to ask for a follow-up meeting after you've done your initial analysis and have determined further specific questions.

Anecdote: I once worked with a fellow who, upon joining the company, took notes like a court stenographer wherever he went during the work day. I would kid him about this, asking when he planned to publish his novel – he filled several pages with writing daily. You could see this technique work for him as his learning curve, in many instances, seemed much shorter than expected. As time went on, his need for note taking lessened, but never went away completely. As I began to copy this tactic, I found my stress level lowering as my brain became directed more towards analysis, and less toward trying to memorize spoken factual information.

Always Recommend a Course of Action

After you dive into an assigned task, alternative approaches can present themselves making you uncertain as to which path to take. *Never* go to your manager simply presenting alternatives expecting him or her to choose the best one. Most managers hate when that happens and can legitimately begin to wonder why they hired you. While they expect you to sometimes ask for their advice, they also expect you to be constantly developing your analytical skills. Here is what you should do in the above situation. Present the various alternatives you are considering to your boss, but be sure to include each alternative's respective pro's and con's as you see them. *Then, most importantly, give your recommended choice and accompanying rationale, even if it is only based on your best guess.* Even if your manager disagrees with your choice and related analysis, he or she will appreciate that you're trying to develop your judgment. You may find this process somewhat painful, at first, but it usually proves to be an efficient way to improve your analytical abilities, as well as learn how your manager thinks. In short order, you will make necessary decisions in confidence without the need to ask your manager's advice.

Raise Warning Flags Early

If you are working to a plan that allocates a certain amount of time per each task, it is essential that you alert your manager as soon as it appears to you that any plan date is in jeopardy. The goal is to eliminate last minute surprises, always making sure that people have as much time as possible to adjust to altered circumstances. If you are constantly waiting until the last minute to inform your manager that more time is needed to complete tasks, he or she will often be put into a difficult situation explaining surprise delays to clients or end-users. Help your manager prepare people for delays by informing him or her as soon as you perceive they will be unavoidable. Early warnings also allow your manager to manage, either by assigning more resources, if available, or otherwise adjusting your workload, possibly allowing you to meet the original plan.

Legal Requirements and Operational Necessities

There are situations when more time is simply not an option, and you will be expected to work the hours necessary to get the job done by the date needed. Such situations fall into two categories: legal requirements and operational necessities. An example of a legal requirement would be passage of a law requiring all of your company's advertising to include a specified written disclaimer by the beginning of the upcoming calendar year. Asking the government for an extension is usually not possible. The needed changes simply must be implemented by January 1st !

Likewise, operational necessities usually won't allow for extensions. The most famous operational necessity of recent times was the so called "Year 2000 date bug." In the early 1990's, everyone who used data processing to support their business, which meant almost everyone, began to realize that most legacy software only allocated two characters to store the year component for most, if not all, dates. The same software usually calculated time spans by simply subtracting one year from the other, such as $75 - 52 = 23$ years. Of course, this would break down as dates beyond the year 1999 became involved in calculations.

A considerable amount of panic swept civilization as people realized that the most extensive software change in history had to be accomplished by 1999! If not, most financial services software, along with much other software, would begin yielding grossly erroneous and possibly dangerous results. Most computer programs had to have year information fields expanded to four characters and corresponding calculations modified to make use of the expanded fields. In this way, 1975 – 1952 would yield the correct number of 23 years, as before, *and* 2018 – 1988 would also yield the correct number of 30 years instead of the previously erroneous calculation of -70 years (18 -88)! Many people, in countless organizations throughout the world, worked long hours during the 1990's to make the needed changes and, for the most part, predicted problems were averted when the year 2000 dawned.

If you work for an organization that releases new products, say, each October as does the automobile industry, your employer will consider such an annual release to be an operational necessity in terms of maintaining a competitive advantage, and won't respond kindly to any request to extend the product release date. Depending on the industry you enter, legal requirements and operational necessities can become a critical part of your working life.

7
Being an Effective Change Agent

The author compares two common change agent strategies along with what understandings must be reached with management in order for them to be effective.

In some entry-level jobs, your manager may expect you to act as a "Change Agent" within your organization. Being the person responsible for catalyzing needed change can be fulfilling and exhilarating, or highly frustrating and stressful, depending on the following conditions. Does senior management know about your Change Agent role? Does senior management fully support you as a Change Agent? Will senior management stand up and endorse your role in front of the people you are being tasked to influence? Even if the answers to the prior questions are all affirmative, you will usually find that you can't begin suggesting new ideas or ways of doing things in the first week or even few months on your new job. You need to discuss this thoroughly with your manager because he or she may actually expect you to voice strong opinions to groups of your peers from day one. However, when you do, other managers and peers may resent and resist you so strongly as to jeopardize any future effectiveness you may have within the organization!

In order to avoid this fate, you may have to educate your managers to the Rawhide Theory of Change Agency. In the 1960's TV Western, Rawhide, which introduced America to Clint Eastwood, there was often a cattle stampede. Cattle, it seems, are easily spooked, just like your co-workers. Inexperienced cowboy "Change Agents" would often ride head-on towards the lead animals in a courageous, but disastrous, attempt to get the herd to immediately change direction and avoid going over the always nearby cliff. The older cowhands knew better. They would begin by riding their horses within the herd for a while in the direction of the cliff, and then, slowly but surely, begin to alter the course of the herd to avoid certain death. Later, they would go back and help recover the remains of the fellows who tried the full frontal assault technique. The lesson for you and your boss is simple. Change Agents often have to go along with the group for a while, gaining understanding of the group and why it may resist change. This holds true regardless of which change agency methodology you adopt (two methodologies are discussed below). Only when mutual understanding and trust are achieved, can a Change Agent begin to effectively introduce new ideas to a new group or organization.

You can be a Change Agent in two basic ways. The first involves more subtlety and finesse, but can bear significant results. I call this strategy the "let them think it was their idea in the first place" approach to Change Agency. This method requires many one-on-one client encounters in which you repeatedly stress the benefits of new approaches. This is combined with actively supporting any of your client's attempts to implement the suggested changes. At some point, you begin to hear your client advocate your recommendations to others, often in ways that are as enthusiastic as when you do it. At that point, you continue to help your client implement the changes he or she is now promoting, all the while crediting him or her with the improved way of doing things. When the client gains success in this way, he or she will be much more receptive to your future suggestions.

Sometimes, usually for political reasons, your boss wants it made clear to everyone that you (and by extension, your boss) are the source of all new ideas. You may be expected to speak up whenever and wherever possible, even if it embarrasses your client. Subtlety is abandoned in exchange for the marketing and promotion of you and your boss. This approach can be effective provided you enjoy strong overt support from senior management.

If you are hired as a Change Agent, it is imperative that you know which of the above methodologies is expected of you. They each have their unique pros and cons, so it is important to communicate clearly about them with your manager prior to implementing either one. Be aware, though, that whichever methodology you choose, results can take time. If management is looking for rapid significant change in an organization, they should be mandating it from senior management down as opposed to having peer Change Agents try to catalyze it from the bottom up.

Anecdote: In the 1990's, I worked within a Change Management team assigned many Change Agency roles within a large company. The first three managers of this team were veteran company employees who had considerable credibility as Change Agents among their peer managers. However, our fourth boss (I'll call him Fred) was a manager hired from a nearby government contractor. Fred was highly self-confident but not great at reading other people. In his very first company-wide Change Management meeting with his new peer managers, he spoke right up several times, even contradicting several people in the room. The looks he got should have told him something about the culture he had entered. However, Fred kept right on going as if he were receiving the most positive feedback and encouragement. Fred never really recovered from that first meeting. He was determined to change the direction of his clients before getting to know them. Like the doomed cowboys on Rawhide, Fred's career with the company was soon being scraped off of the home office floor. Fortunately for Fred, his prior employer had a place for him to return to within the year.

Anecdote: During the 1990's, while working within the team mentioned in the above anecdote, I practiced the "let them think it was their idea in the first place" approach to Change Agency with considerable success. This approach fit my personality and was endorsed by my managers. In 2002, I took a position in another division of the same company which also required me to be a Change Agent. However, this time I was expected to make it clear at every possible opportunity that I was the source of all new ideas. After years of persuading behind the scenes, I found it very difficult to begin conducting mini-lectures to my client managers in the middle of open meetings. I got better doing this over time, but really had to work at it.

8

Peers and Other Managers

This chapter contains a discussion of human nature in relation to life and workplace pressures. What motivates people in the workplace and why caution is advised regarding discussing or trusting co-workers and managers.

Many of your co-workers will see you as a valuable resource and ally in the ongoing battle to achieve the organization's goals, and will try to help you succeed whenever possible in a true spirit of teamwork. These people, usually the majority, will be a joy to work with. However, other co-workers will see you solely as a competitor for finite salary dollars and promotions. Within this latter group are individuals who feel tremendous pressure to succeed at all costs, either because of their feelings of insecurity, extreme ambition, or external pressures such as financial indebtedness, or providing food and shelter for their families. Sadly, you may find yourself dealing with a co-worker who believes that all is fair in this world, and that only one of you is going to look good to management when evaluation time roles around. Some individuals, who otherwise wish you no harm, will, at times, be unwilling to share information which they acquired only after considerable pain and effort. Others will equate knowledge to power and thereby keep what they know largely to themselves. You need to be able to judge which people are dealing with you in good faith and which are not. Towards this end, you need to develop relationships with as many co-workers and managers as possible. In so doing, you will hear many opinions about the various people that you work with. You need to balance those opinions against your personal experiences and come to your own conclusions regarding the level of trust you should give each of your co-workers. The best approach to developing a solid reputation among your co-workers and managers is to be helpful and positive to everyone at all times, while being clinically objective about which individuals are likely to reciprocate when you are in need of assistance.

Listen to what people say about each other, but avoid disclosing your opinions regarding co-workers and managers, especially when new to an organization. You never know who may be within earshot over a cubicle wall, or sitting at the other end of a speaker phone. Even if you are outside of the workplace, the person you confide in regarding a co-worker or manager can, wittingly or unwittingly, pass on your comments to others who may have a relationship with the individual you discussed. Most successful individuals rarely, if ever, disclose strong feelings regarding co-workers other than to say that they like working with everyone! You need to reserve your trust for co-workers and managers only after several experiences over time provide you with ample evidence that a person has earned your trust. At the same time, you need to be open to the ever-present possibility that you have misunderstood an individual's actions or intentions. Also, people can change over time for good or ill. Obviously, all of this takes patience, discretion, and an ongoing effort on your part to keep an open mind regarding everyone that you come into contact with.

Anecdote: Early in my career, I worked next to a man who constantly gave phone callers a really hard time. Rude and demanding, he often raised his voice and even, on occasion, hung-up on people! While he wasn't on my team, I couldn't help but hear his tirades through the cubicle wall. One day, management announced that we were no longer to allow this fellow into the building, as he was no longer working for the company. A few weeks later, he was seen on local television, in handcuffs, being arrested for killing his girlfriend, a crime for which he was subsequently convicted! This rather extreme experience taught me that you can never be too careful getting to know the people you meet at work. In this case, the individual constantly betrayed his malevolence by his actions. However, there will be many other instances in your career when a potential back-stabber will exhibit a ready smile and a friendly manner.

Anecdote: Having newly joined a company, my manager assigned me a technical mentor to help me become productive on a major project. This fellow was marvelous. He either readily gave me needed information or knew where I could obtain it. I could tell that he wanted me to succeed, and consequently I felt nothing but good will towards him. One day, I encountered this fellow coming into work. He seemed very different, talking a mile-a-minute and looking agitated. I later learned he had recently popped off in a meeting, basically telling a couple of senior managers where they could go! The next day, when this fellow was not in the building, the team manager told us that this man was manic depressive and had stopped taking his medication, which resulted in his bizarre behavior. We were further told that he would be on leave for a while, but to expect him back once he had gotten himself together. When he did return, everyone did their best to help him feel at home back on our team. It seems he had a history of being as helpful to others as he had been to me, and people were more than happy to show him generosity in return. The lesson is simple: you reap what you sow. (NOTE: in today's environment of extreme confidentiality, it is unlikely management would discuss the medical status of an employee, as was done above, with the employee's peers. While there are good reasons for this, the preceding anecdote illustrates what positive effects can be lost.)

Most organizations, big and small, have a rumor mill. Occasionally, but very rarely, a rumor is actually true. Most often they are off base, if not totally false. The best approach to the rumor mill is to take every rumor you hear with a very large grain of salt. You will go crazy, otherwise, worrying about things that will probably never happen, or were never true to begin with. At team meetings, managers often ask, "Has anyone heard any good rumors lately?" This is often an attempt to deal with rumors before they get out of hand. Usually, a manager can simply knock down the rumor with facts, or explain how the rumor got started. Occasionally, a manager will actually verify a rumor, but that doesn't happen often!

Anecdote: During a time of layoffs within the company, the rumor quickly spread that the portrait paintings of prior CEOs had been removed from their locations on the first floor of the main entrance rotunda and put into storage as part of a program to promote a more youthful corporate image. After about a week of hearing this, I took a walk to the rotunda to see for myself. The paintings had indeed been removed from their normal locations. When I remarked about this, the receptionist told me to go to the upper level of the rotunda where I encountered all the portraits re-hung in full view of all who walked by. They had been moved, I learned, in hopes that they would be better preserved away from the constantly opening outer doors near their prior locations on the lower level.

9
Conflict Management

Many times in your career, but particularly in the beginning, you will have to manage conflict from a position of little or no power.

The first time you find yourself in a conflict with a peer or other manager, be sure you know how your management, or in the case of a union shop, your union representative wants you to proceed. Unions usually have highly detailed dispute resolution procedures for you to follow, and your union rep will usually be able to help you through the process. In the following example, I am discussing a non-union environment, but the concepts involved can be helpful in many different situations.

Go to your manager and lay out the problem that you are having. After reviewing the ways you are considering to address the problem, ask your manager if he or she can give you any insights regarding your issue, or suggestions regarding how you might deal with the person in question. Your manager may provide you with his or her insight, suggest a course of action, or tell you that you need to modify your own behavior or attitude. Sometimes, a manager will want to meet with you and the other person in an attempt to mediate the issue. However, most managers are time stressed and otherwise hate dealing with conflicts between subordinates. They usually request that you first try to work out the problem, as best you can, directly with the person in question.

In that case, you need to evaluate whether a one-on-one meeting with the person would likely result in constructive communication. Is this person an honest individual who deals with people in good faith? If not, you may decide to pass on contacting the person and, instead, consider ways to minimize your interactions with him or her, if that's at all possible (see the following Anecdote).

If you decide to proceed with a meeting, you should first review the subtopic "Telling it Like it is - Assertive Communication and Behaviors" (see page 21). Consider whether meeting with the person behind closed doors is a wise thing to do. Sometimes, a meeting in a corner of the cafeteria, or other semi-public space, will allow a degree of privacy while discouraging the other person from engaging in aggressive or bullying behaviors. Remember, your reputation with existing managers and any potential managers within the organization is everything. Is the person you are meeting with either a manager, potential manager, or a friend or relative of your manager or any other manager in the company? If they are, you need to be extra careful in how you deal with him or her.

Your goal in the meeting is to assertively make clear to the other person what he or she is doing that causes you a problem, and to explain to the person exactly why their action(s), or inaction(s), are an issue for you. *Stick to discussing behaviors rather than speculating about the other person's motivations.* You can't advance to discussing next steps until you obtain at least an understanding of this first part by the other person. He or she may fully acknowledge your perception, but still not agree that you have a legitimate issue. In this case, you may have to end the meeting, agreeing to disagree, while hopefully having each gained some understanding of the other's point of view. While not totally satisfying, this isn't necessarily a bad result, and can lead to easier times between the two of you. The most satisfying meeting also involves discussion and agreement on either bilateral or unilateral behavioral changes aimed at resolving the problem in question. Never assume a tone of victory in such an outcome. Express thanks to the other person for meeting with you and say how much you look forward to working with him or her down the road. When you next see your manager, he or she may ask for a summary of the meeting. Whether you report a highly successful outcome, or something less, let your manager suggest your next action(s) if he or she chooses to do so. As in other realms of human relations, there is sometimes no clear-cut immediately satisfying resolution to workplace conflict. Often patience, ongoing communication, and good will are required on a day-by-day basis, keeping your long-term goals and interests in mind.

Anecdote: Having newly joined the company, my manager assigned me a technical mentor to help me become productive on a major project. However, actually locating this person to get information was a real challenge. As she was usually away from her desk, I would leave notes on her chair, asking her to call me when she had a few minutes. When we did interact, my mentor seemed less than interested in my information needs. When days would pass with no mentor response, I would explain the situation to my manager who likewise seemed unsympathetic saying that I had to work things out with the mentor by myself. Finally, I learned that the mentor and my manager were close friends who often saw each other socially. I realized anything that sounded like a complaint regarding my so-called mentor was going to fall on deaf ears. It was also clear, from what I had heard about my mentor, that she was a person who was not prone to share information and tended to portray co-workers as incompetent. I stopped wasting time seeking out this person and began to develop other sources of information. This experience quickly taught me that 1) not all designated mentors want to be mentors, 2) you never know what personal relationships underlie your company's organization chart, and 3) sometimes going around a problem is the wisest approach, especially when dealing with people who are not dealing with you in good faith.

10

A Few Miscellaneous Issues

The author discusses how you should approach several important topics whether or not they are addressed in your organization's employee manual.

Clothing: No matter what style of clothes you wear, always dress neatly. It's best to dress as your peers do – the workplace is not the place for individual fashion statements which can subconsciously alienate you from your co-workers. When in doubt, it's best to dress up rather then dress down. If your goal is to become a manager, seriously consider dressing in traditional formal business attire at all times. This sends an unmistakable signal to your boss supplementing what you should be telling him or her about your career goals. You can find many excellent internet web sites on this topic by searching the phrase "dress for success".

Anecdote: When I began my career in data processing, the issue of appropriate workplace attire was often discussed. Some of my peers thought that formal dress had absolutely no psychological effect on people, and the notion that it ever did was simply old thinking. I decided to do an experiment. I needed to return a dress shirt to a local department store. The last time I did so, about a year earlier, I went to the store in a polo shirt, shorts and tennis shoes. I was able to return the shirt, but only after a few questions about why I was returning the article and would I like a store credit or to exchange for another size or color. This time, I put on a dark grey suit, striped shirt with necktie, and black dress shoes. I approached the service desk announcing that I was returning a shirt. The clerk took one look at me and said, "no problem". No questions were asked and the whole transaction took a fraction of the time of the prior year's return.

Profanity: Using profanity of any kind is never a good idea. It lessens the impact of your ideas and diminishes your respect among co-workers.

Sarcasm: Using sarcasm of any kind is never a good idea. It lessens the impact of your ideas and diminishes your respect among co-workers.

Religion / Politics: One of the most common aphorisms regarding the workplace is to avoid discussing religion and politics. This is because it's both wise and true. You can waste a lot of time, and withdraw heavily from your co-workers emotional bank accounts, by discussing / arguing about issues within these two broad topics – issues which people are emotionally vested in, and not likely to change their opinions about.

Humor: For the most part, you should avoid telling jokes or funny stories in the workplace, especially early on in your employment. If you must, a little self deprecating humor (humor in which you are the butt of the joke) can sometimes be in order. However, be aware that humor is highly subjective. What makes one person laugh can be highly offensive and even hurtful to the next person. Your joke about a traveling salesman may offend the woman two cubicles down whose father was a traveling salesman. You never know how a joke, no matter how gentle, strikes the listener, or what may be going on in the listener's life at any given moment. If you feel humor is an important part of your personality, at least take the time to really know your audience before you indulge. If you are at all in doubt about the appropriateness of what you are about to say, don't say it!

Anecdote: A vice president was giving a presentation to his boss, the company's new Chief Information Officer. This fellow definitely had a mischievous side. To introduce a software utility called "Flasher", he used a drawing of the rear-view of a man holding his trench coat open! Within days, everyone in the division heard that the new CIO was far from amused, which explained the subsequent shrinkage of the vice presidents duties. If this unfortunate fellow had waited until he gained more familiarity with his new boss, he probably would have passed on his questionable choice in humor.

Nicknames: As a new employee, you often have to be flexible regarding your role in the organization. Even the newest member on the United States Supreme Court has to tend the door at meetings. However, some items are non-negotiable. The only nicknames anyone should refer to you by are ones that you approve of. Everyone has the right to be called only by whatever name(s) they want to be called. For example, I go by "Rich" or "Richard". I dislike being called "Dick" or "Rick", and tell people so whenever they try using those nicknames, or any other. If you want to be called only "Elizabeth", don't hesitate to let people know of your displeasure at being called "Babs", "Beth", or "Betty". Like-wise, don't refer to anyone by a nickname until you've asked them for their approval, "do you prefer James or is Jim OK?" Be aware that some people don't like their given legal name and prefer to always be called by something else!

Physical Contact: Avoid physical contact with your co-workers. The main exception is a handshake, when appropriate, which should be firm and brief. Don't hesitate to take a person aside, including a manager, and tell him or her of your desire not to be touched if he or she has been too familiar. One other exception can be when your boss is introducing or praising you to other people with his or her hand lightly on your shoulder or arm.

Gender Speak: Avoid using "girls", "gals", or "boys" when referring to co-workers. Use "men" and "women" or "gentlemen" and "ladies".

Anecdote: A friend of mine began a job in the private sector after many years of teaching high school. He enjoyed his new co-workers, but told me of his puzzlement regarding cold looks he'd receive when referring to some of his female colleagues as "girls", as in, "are you girls coming to the meeting?" I asked him if he would like being referred to as a "boy" in front of his co-workers. I reminded my friend that no matter how young they seemed to him, these women likely had goals of advancement within the company and that no one makes a "girl" a vice president. When put in that context, my friend could understand his co-workers' reactions.

Vacation Ethic: Employers often allow employees to carry a certain number of vacation days over to the next year and/or cash in a certain number of unused vacation days on a regular basis. Avoid accumulating unused vacation days. Think about when you want to use them and put those dates in your weekly statuses as soon as you are aware of them. Account for upcoming vacation days in your project plans. The best way to maintain a high level of productivity is to enjoy your full allotment of vacation each year so that your batteries are fully recharged when you are at work (see **Work Ethic**).

Work Ethic: Be on-time to work and while there give 100%. It is always better to put in a busy eight hour day than to spread eight hours of work over ten hours of physical presence. Do your best to accommodate your employer's unforeseen needs such as overtime to meet legal requirements, operational necessities, or a client's last minute changes. There will be times when you will have a short notice need for time off due to a sick child or a surprise houseguest. Most employers will gladly accommodate you, if you have been taking care of them. Only take sick days when you are actually sick. If you need an "attitude adjustment day", take a vacation day.

Age Speak: Sometimes, professional people refer to co-workers under thirty, or so, as "kids". This is usually a term of endearment not intended to demean anyone. On the other hand, avoid using the terms "boys" or "girls" when referring to colleagues. Also, it is never wise to refer to an older co-worker as a "dinosaur" or similar term highlighting someone's advancing years.

11

Benefits and Responsibilities

A brief overview of several topics likely addressed in Corporate Employee Manuals followed by a detailed discussion of Cash Value, Defined Benefit, and Defined Contribution retirement plans. Roth IRAs are also discussed.

Does your company publish a Corporate Employee Manual? If yes, make sure to obtain a copy for your reference. Review this manual and become familiar with its contents. Most organizations have policies regarding the following topics, either contained within various employee publications, or available from corporate human resources, or your supervisor.

Dress Code: Some dress codes are highly specific. Many are quite vague. In the latter instance, you need to rely on your immediate supervisor for advice.

Discrimination: How does your company define unlawful discrimination? Does your company recognize all forms of unlawful discrimination regarding gender, race, sexual orientation, age?

Harassment Policy: How does your company define Sexual Harassment? Does your company recognize other forms of harassment in the workplace?

Intellectual Property Rights: If you create a new product or idea while working for the company or organization, even if outside of regular business hours, who owns the product / idea? Have you signed any documents regarding rights to intellectual property?

Sick Days: Be sure you know how you accrue sick days. Many companies require written documentation from your physician after you are out sick more than a specified number of work days running. Also, short-term and long-term disability can become an issue after you are out sick more than specified lengths of time.

Vacation Days: How do you accrue vacation days? Can you borrow ahead on them (usually decided between you and your manager)? Can you carry any over from year to year, or must vacation days accrued during a year be taken in that year? Can you be paid for any unused vacation days?

Medical and Disability Benefits: What options for medical and disability benefits are available to you, and at what costs? Options are usually presented annually for you to choose from.

Dental and Eye Care Benefits: What options are available to you for dental and eye care benefits, and at what costs? Options are usually presented annually for you to choose from.

Retirement Plans: Even though you are at the beginning of your career, you need to become familiar with your company's retirement plan. How your company's plan is designed can be a factor in how long you decide to stay with the company. Further, its design may sometimes depend on you to make elections and decisions within the plan in order to optimize its benefit to you when you do retire. Neglecting these decisions now can result in considerable financial pain in your latter years.

Three basic types of company sponsored plans – Cash Value, Defined Benefit and Defined Contribution - are discussed below. My intention is not to tell you everything you need to know about retirement planning, but rather provide an overview that can allow you to begin an intelligent conversation with your employer, financial advisor and / or tax accountant.

Cash Value retirement plans have become popular with employers in recent years. In these plans, your employer contributes actual dollars to an account in your name. Each year's contribution is based on your current salary and length of service with the company. If you leave the company, you take the money in your account with you to your next job. Cash Value dollars are pre-tax dollars. That is, provided you roll these dollars into your next employer's Cash Value account in your name, you avoid any tax consequences on the money until, of course, the day you actually retire. What happens then I'll leave to your accountant to explain to you! Cash Value plans tend to provide bigger employer contributions in earlier years of employment than prior types of plans did. These plans require no decision making on your part, at least until retirement. You simply watch the dollars accrue to you over time.

Defined Benefit retirement plans still exist, but are becoming increasingly hard to find. These plans provide you with a guaranteed monthly payment for life upon retirement, based on the average salary you are paid in your final years of service with the company, and the total number of years you worked for the company. You must work a minimum specified number of years with the company to receive this benefit. Usually, the benefit accrues most rapidly during your initial twenty-five, or so, years of service and less rapidly thereafter. Like the Cash Value plan described above, Defined Benefit Plans only require you to make decisions regarding benefit disbursements upon your retirement. Defined Benefit Plans are generally thought to encourage longer stays of employment with companies than Cash Value Plans do.

Defined Contribution retirement plans, also called 401K or 403B plans, require the most administration on the part of employers and the most day-to-day involvement on the part of employees. These plans can be offered in concert with the above plan types or alone. In a Defined Contribution retirement plan, you can take up to a specified percentage of your paycheck and shelter it from immediate taxation by having it invested in any number of investment options offered within the plan by your employer. The investment options can include a guaranteed non-equity fixed return fund, various bond funds, and various kinds of non-guaranteed equity investments such as stocks, mutual funds, etc. Any dollars accrued as investment income remain sheltered from taxation until you reach age 70. Then, you must begin making regular minimum specified withdrawals from both your accrued payroll contributions and any investment returns. By the time you reach retirement, you will likely be in a lower tax bracket, allowing you to keep more of your money than if you had allowed it to be taxed when originally earned. You can withdraw dollars from the plan at any time. However, there is a stiff tax penalty for withdrawing dollars from Defined Contribution retirement plans prior to age 59½. Hardship early withdrawals are sometimes allowed without such penalties. The regulations governing hardship withdrawals change over time, and need to be discussed with your plan's administrator.

You usually need to be employed for a minimum specified number of months with a given employer before you are eligible to participate in the employer's Defined Contribution retirement plan. Once you elect to participate in the plan, you make your initial investment choices, telling the plan administrator which investment options you want your contributions to be divided amongst. Going forward, you can change your investment options on a regular basis regarding money already in the plan, and future contributions. A highly valuable feature of most Defined Contributions plans is the employer's matching contribution. Many employers will match some part, or all, of your initial few percentages of your payroll contributions to the plan (often up to 3%, sometimes more). If your employer matches plan contributions, you should definitely begin making at least the minimum contribution needed to acquire the maximum match as soon as you can. You will be amazed at how rapidly you're Defined Contribution plan dollars will grow, while shrinking your take-home pay less than you might expect!

Remember, you are taking dollars from your paycheck and putting them into the plan each pay period. This decreases the amount of taxes that need to be deducted from your paycheck, while gaining matching employer dollars within your plan account! Once most people understand this, they begin increasing their percentage of overall contributions to their Defined Contribution plans as soon as they can, usually once a house down payment has been saved. People who "max out" their Defined Contribution plan contributions early in their careers, and make needed investment option changes over the years, usually have a very healthy plan balance once they reach retirement. Some Defined Contribution plans allow you to also contribute after tax / non-tax sheltered salary dollars to plan investment accounts. Government regulations specify maximum contributions regarding both pre-tax and after-tax dollars made to Defined Contribution plans within a given year. Dollars from prior employer's Defined Contribution plans can be rolled over into any new employer's Defined Contribution plan if you move to a new job.

Roth IRA: Whether or not you max out your Defined Contribution retirement plan contributions, you can often invest more of your after tax dollars in a government sponsored retirement vehicle known as a Roth IRA. In this form of Individual Retirement Account, you can contribute up to a specified amount of after tax dollars (no pre-tax dollars allowed) each year in any number of investment options offered by the financial institution administering your Roth IRA. Unlike a Defined Contribution retirement plan, a Roth IRA allows you to withdraw after tax *contributions* at any time without penalty. However, like an employer's Defined Contribution retirement plan, a Roth IRA does not allow for early pre-retirement withdrawals of *investment returns*. The good – many would say, great - news is that when you do begin your Roth IRA retirement withdrawals, you incur absolutely no income tax liabilities! You've already paid taxes on your contributions, and a Roth IRA's investment earnings are, by law, *tax free* to you! Because of this, many financial advisors tell clients to put their money into a Roth IRA before considering putting dollars into a Defined Contribution (401K / 403B) retirement plan. Roth IRAs can be set up through various financial institutions and are available to any individual, whether working for someone else, or self-employed.

12
Independent Contractors

Are you an employee or an independent contractor? Independent Contractors are defined and discussed in terms of Internal Revenue Service regulations.

Independent Contractors are self-employed individuals who contract to provide deliverables and / or services to companies, non-profits, government bodies, or other individuals. Independent Contractors provide for their own benefits and pay their own social security taxes. A true independent contractor is given the end-goal or requirements for a desired deliverable and decides for himself or herself how to fulfill the goal, or produce the deliverable. The Internal Revenue Service uses several criteria in deciding Independent Contractor status. These criteria change almost yearly, but usually include the following. Does the individual...

- work in a building provided by the employer and use employer provided office supplies?
- attend regular staff meetings which include regular employees of the employer?
- produce services or deliverables according to employer mandated procedures?
- work for a set number of hours a week as required by the employer?
- receive benefits from the employer beyond monetary compensation for services rendered?

An answer of "yes" to one or more of the above does not necessarily result in the IRS rejecting Independent Contractor status. The decision is made on a case-by-case basis and can sometimes appear arbitrary to an outside observer. To avoid confusion and costly misunderstandings, it is always best for employers and independent contractors to deal with each other within the terms and conditions of a well written contract.

13
Leaving the Job

While it may seem counterintuitive to some, how you leave a job can be just as important as how you obtain and hold one.

No one can tell you when you should leave a job. Only you can decide that for yourself. There are as many reasons to leave a job as there are reasons for working in the first place. If you decide to leave for non job related reasons such as family issues, a desire to see a different part of the country, or simply because you have found a better job in the same or a different field, make it clear to your current management that nothing was a problem at work, and disclose what your move is about. Most managers will understand, wish you success, and keep you in mind should you apply to return in the future. If management thinks you are unhappy with your job, they are less likely to consider you, should you seek to return down the road.

If, on the other hand, you are considering leaving your job because you have a problem, or problems, with the job, I recommend taking the following actions before handing in your notice. First, have a frank discussion with your manager about your issues, and see if there is any way things can change to allow you to stay in your current position. If not, are there other positions within the company that might better suit you? Does the company have an internal job post system that you can use to explore alternatives? Consider speaking with middle and senior managers regarding your concerns and whether circumstances could change to allow you to stay. Whatever you do, never issue an ultimatum such as, "Either I get to work in Graphic Services, or I'm out of here!" Most people will respond by asking you not to slam the door on your way out! At most, say that you'd really like to work in Graphic Services and hope that you can do so within the company. The message is clear that you are seriously considering leaving the company to pursue your goal, but not in a way that makes management feel bullied. You want everyone to feel there is room for civil discussion / negotiation.

If all else fails and you decide that it is really time to leave the company, do not hand in your notice until you have secured an offer for your next job *in writing*. This is the number one rule for financial survival in today's work environment – a rule that, when ignored, can result in considerable pain and hardship. Unfortunately, jobs offered verbally can fall through once you decide to accept. Do not put yourself out on the street unemployed – get that job offer in writing!

In all cases, avoid burning bridges or otherwise settling scores before you leave. You never know if you will one day want to return to the company, or, if a co-worker will follow you to your next, or a future job! No matter what your profession, remember that you belong to a professional community. Some day, that person you worked with in Boston may join your new company in Seattle!

No matter how you feel about the company you are leaving, you want to leave as amicably and gracefully as possible.

Anecdote: Upon leaving a company where I had worked for several years, I went to an exit interview at the request of the Human Resources department. Such interviews are usually fairly routine affairs in which the soon-to-be former employee is asked about his or her experiences with the company, and if he or she felt the company needed to change anything. At the end of the interview, as we stood to shake hands, the interviewer looked me in the eye and said, "Well, Roger, we're really going to miss you around here!" In spite of the fact that my name wasn't Roger, I thanked him and quietly left the building.

About the Author

Richard LaPalme's early interests in the biological sciences led him to attain a National Science Foundation Graduate Fellowship Honorable Mention in 1975 for work in genetics at the University of New Hampshire. As creator and head of Spalding Sporting Goods' entry-level IT training program in the early 1980's, he combined his Masters in Education from Springfield College with his experiences as a teaching tennis professional to begin mentoring new employees on how to successfully transition from academia to the work world. Richard continued mentoring employees in various contexts throughout the remainder of his twenty-seven year career at Farm Credit Banks and Massachusetts Mutual Life Insurance Company. He resides today in the town of Agawam in Western Massachusetts.

19818578R00048

Made in the USA
Lexington, KY
08 January 2013